PIANO

T0052402

ESCAPADES

From the DreamWorks Film CATCH ME IF YOU CAN

Solo Alto Saxophone with Piano Reduction

JOHN WILLIAMS

DREAMWORKS
DREAMWORKS/SKG MUSIC™

**DreamWorks
PICTURES**™

A Publication of

cherry lane
music company

Exclusively Distributed By

HAL•LEONARD®
CORPORATION
7777 W. BLUEMOUND RD. P.O. BOX 13819 MILWAUKEE, WI 53213

The 2002 film *Catch Me If You Can* constituted a delightful departure for director Steven Spielberg. It tells the story of Frank Abagnale, the teenaged imposter, who baffled FBI agents with his incredible exploits.

The film is set in the now nostalgically tinged 1960's, and so it seemed to me that I might evoke the atmosphere of that time by writing a sort of impressionistic memoir of the progressive jazz movement that was then so popular. The alto saxophone seemed the ideal vehicle for this expression and the three movements of this suite are the result.

In "Closing In," we have music that relates to the often humorous sleuthing which took place in the story, followed by "Reflections," which refers to the fragile relationships in Abagnale's broken family. Finally, in "Joy Ride," we have the music that accompanied Frank's wild flights of fantasy that took him all around the world before the law finally reigned him in.

In recording the soundtrack for this entertaining film, I had the services of saxophonist Dan Higgins, to whom I'm indebted for his virtuosic skill and beautiful sound. My greatest reward would be if other players of this elegant instrument might find some joy in this music.

John Williams

From The DreamWorks Film CATCH ME IF YOU CAN

ESCAPADES

JOHN WILLIAMS

1. Closing In

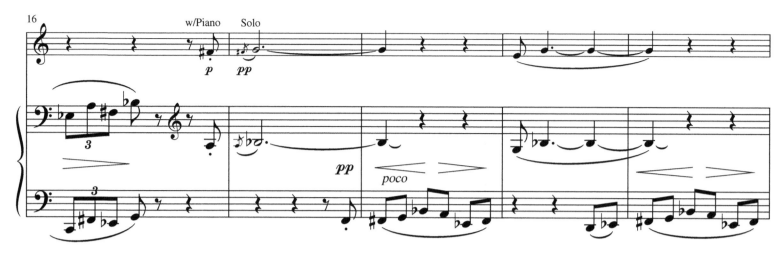

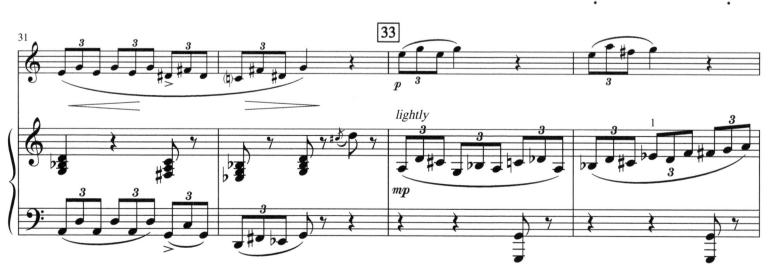

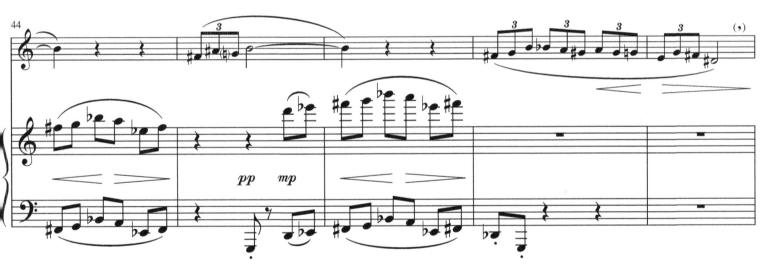

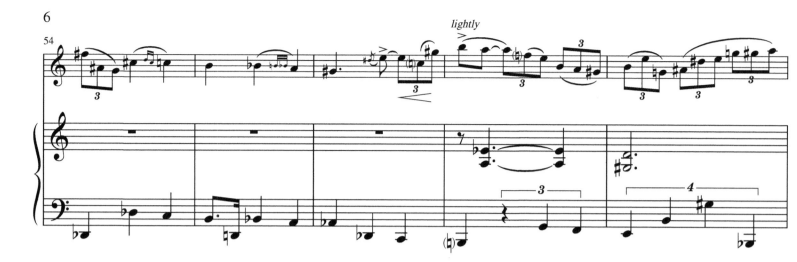

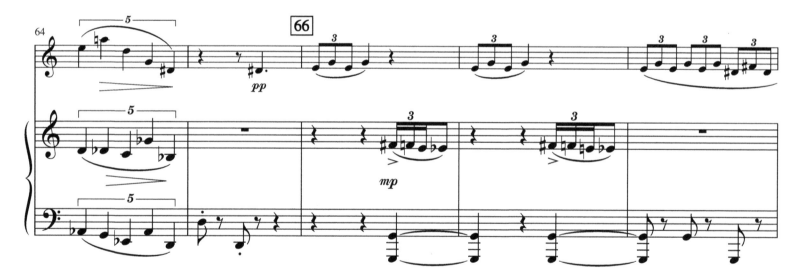

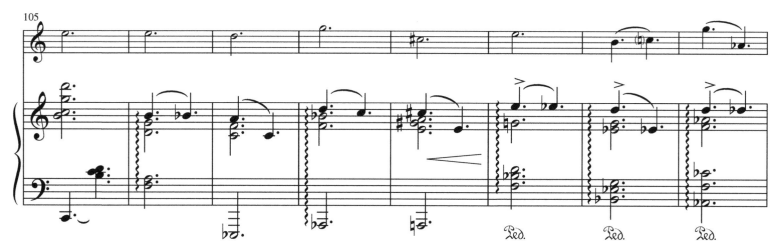

2. Reflections

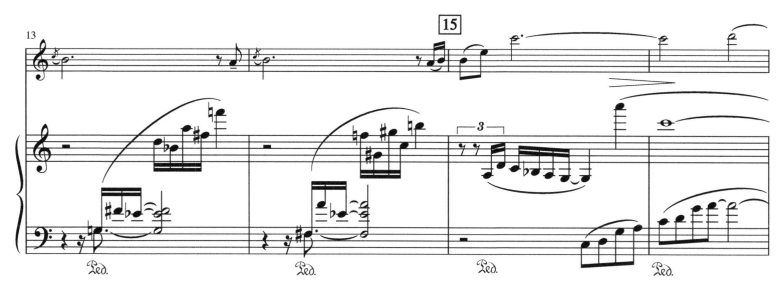

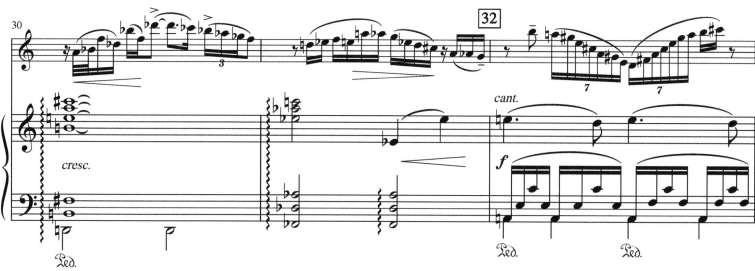

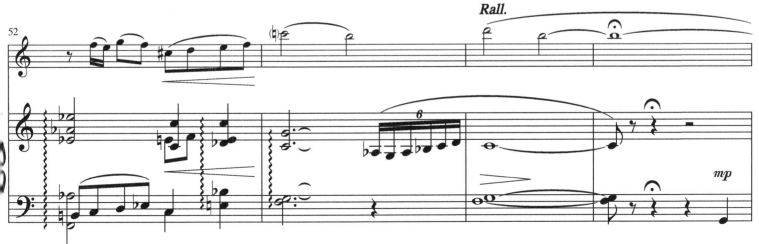

14

Cadenza

Colla parte

Slowly & Reflectively

Cadenza

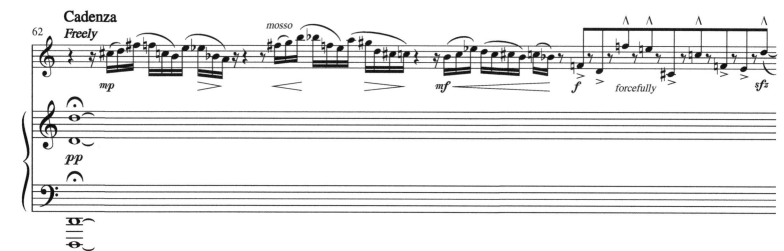

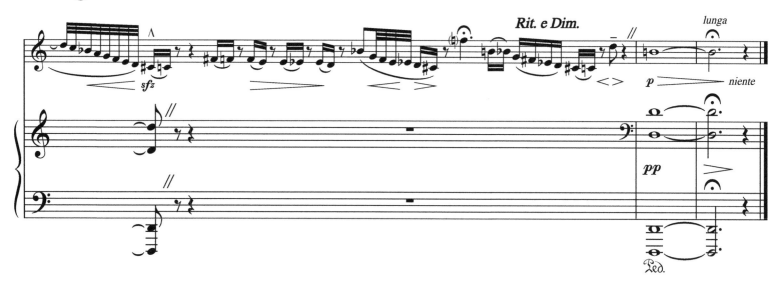

Eb ALTO SAXOPHONE

ESCAPADES

From the DreamWorks Film CATCH ME IF YOU CAN

Solo Alto Saxophone with Piano Reduction

JOHN WILLIAMS

A Publication of

cherry lane
music company

EXCLUSIVELY DISTRIBUTED BY
HAL•LEONARD®
CORPORATION
7777 W. BLUEMOUND RD. P.O. BOX 13819 MILWAUKEE, WI 53213

The 2002 film *Catch Me If You Can* constituted a delightful departure for director Steven Spielberg. It tells the story of Frank Abagnale, the teenaged imposter, who baffled FBI agents with his incredible exploits.

The film is set in the now nostalgically tinged 1960's, and so it seemed to me that I might evoke the atmosphere of that time by writing a sort of impressionistic memoir of the progressive jazz movement that was then so popular. The alto saxophone seemed the ideal vehicle for this expression and the three movements of this suite are the result.

In "Closing In," we have music that relates to the often humorous sleuthing which took place in the story, followed by "Reflections," which refers to the fragile relationships in Abagnale's broken family. Finally, in "Joy Ride," we have the music that accompanied Frank's wild flights of fantasy that took him all around the world before the law finally reigned him in.

In recording the soundtrack for this entertaining film, I had the services of saxophonist Dan Higgins, to whom I'm indebted for his virtuosic skill and beautiful sound. My greatest reward would be if other players of this elegant instrument might find some joy in this music.

John Williams

4

ESCAPADES

E♭ ALTO SAXOPHONE

JOHN WILLIAMS

1. Closing In

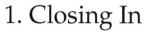

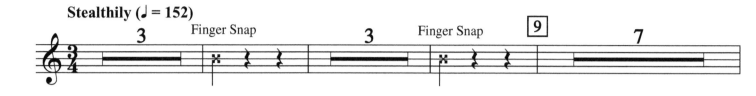

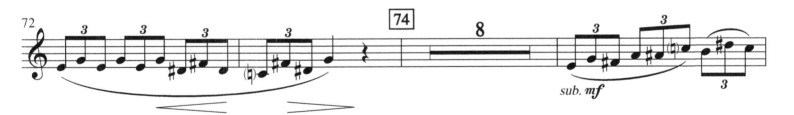

2. Reflections

Reflectively & freely

accel. ad lib.

Moderato (Nostalgically)

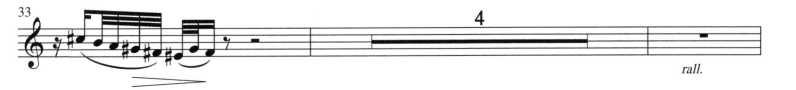

3. Joy Ride

Joyfully, with quiet expectation (♩ = 134)

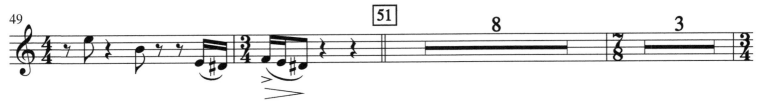

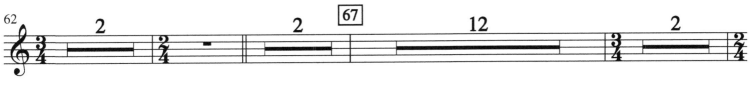

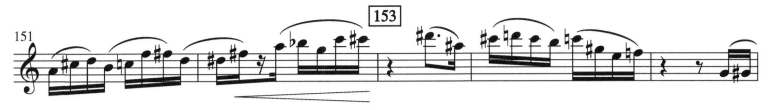

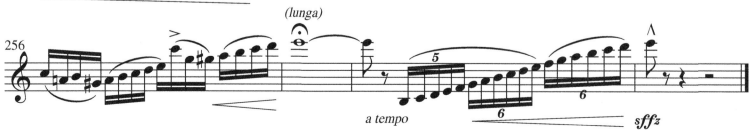

3. Joy Ride

Joyfully, with quiet expectation (♩ = 134)

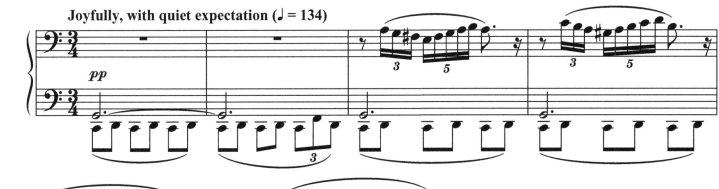

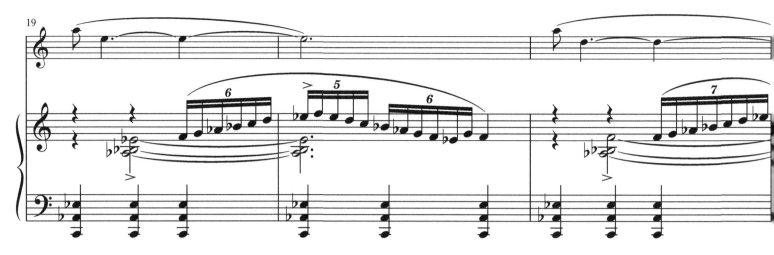

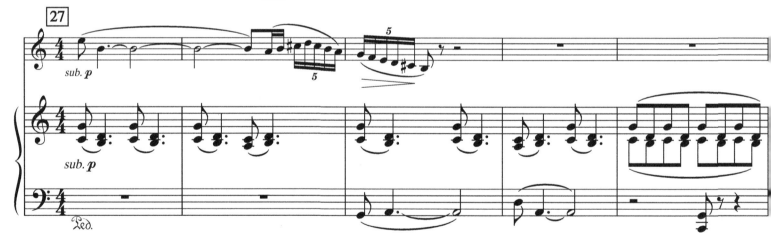

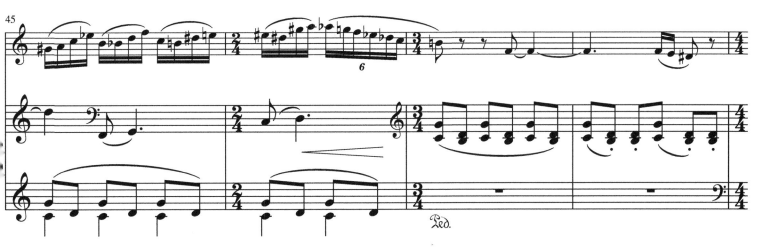

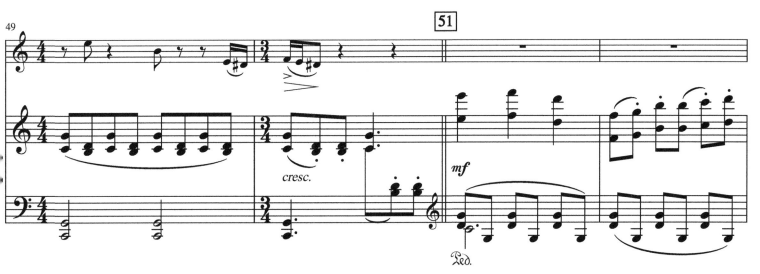

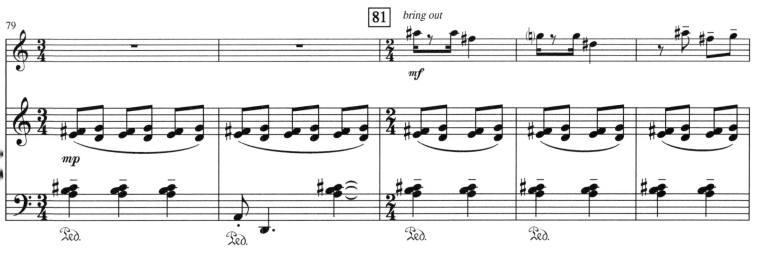

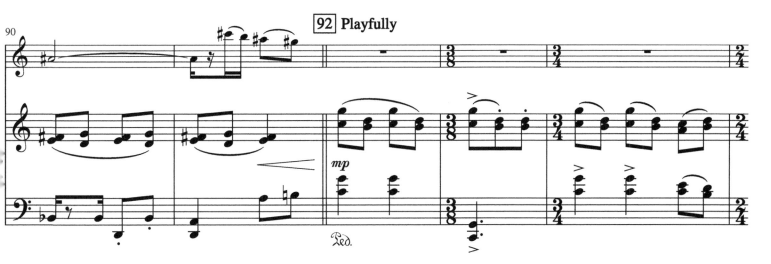

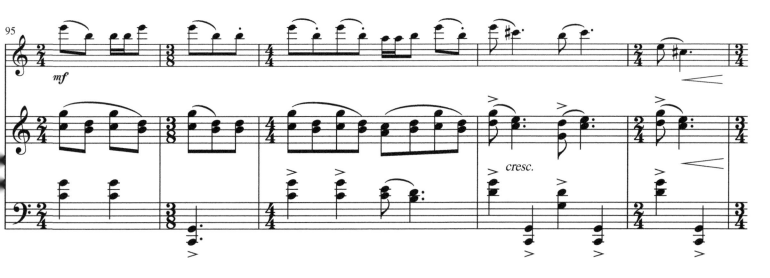

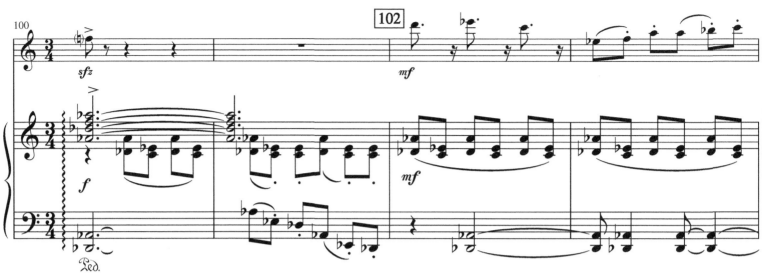

21

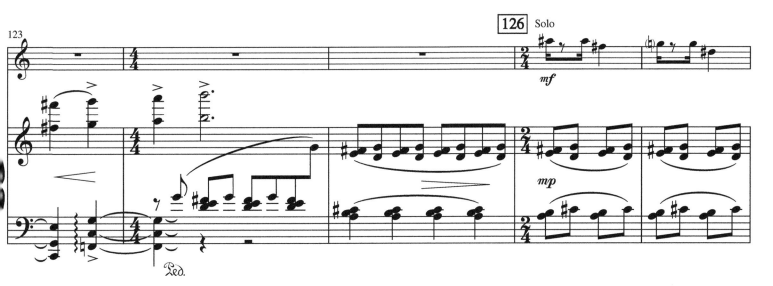

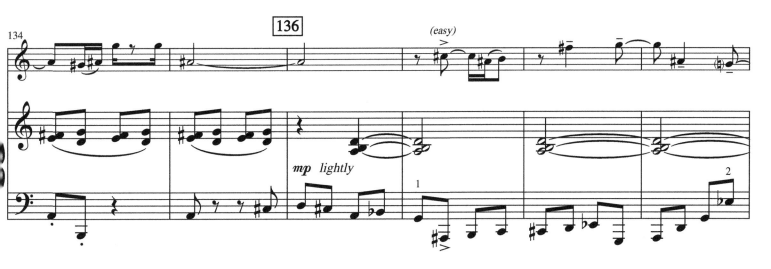

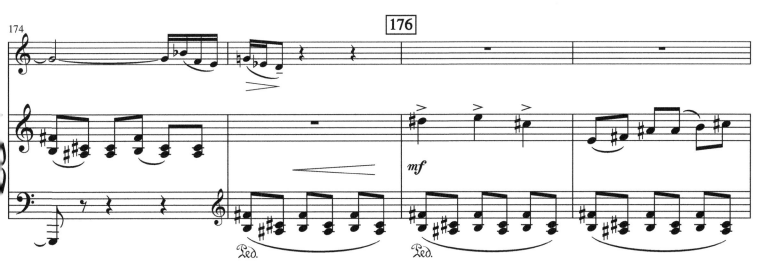

24

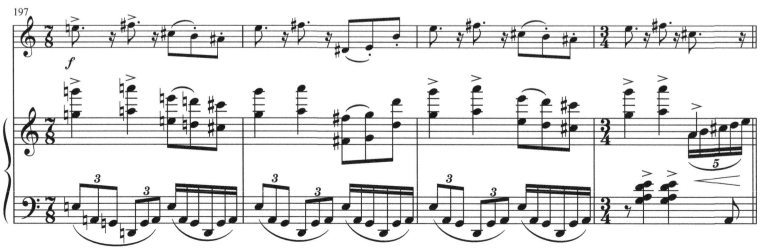

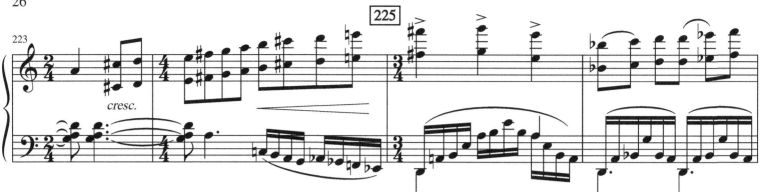

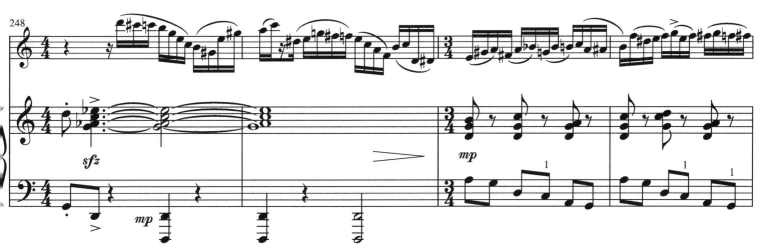